THIS BOOK BELONGS TO

_____

_____

START DATE _____/_____/_____

## HE READS TRUTH

### EXECUTIVE

**FOUNDER /
CHIEF EXECUTIVE OFFICER**
Raechel Myers

**CO-FOUNDER /
CHIEF CONTENT OFFICER**
Amanda Bible Williams

**CHIEF OPERATING OFFICER**
Ryan Myers

**EXECUTIVE ASSISTANT**
Sarah Andereck

### EDITORIAL

**EDITORIAL DIRECTOR**
Jessica Lamb

**MANAGING EDITOR**
Beth Joseph

**CONTENT EDITOR**
Kara Gause

**ASSOCIATE EDITORS**
Bailey Gillespie
Tameshia Williams

**EDITORIAL ASSISTANT**
Hannah Little

### MARKETING

**MARKETING MANAGER**
Katie Matuska Pierce

**COMMUNITY SUPPORT SPECIALIST**
Margot Williams

### CREATIVE

**CREATIVE DIRECTOR**
Jeremy Mitchell

**LEAD DESIGNER**
Kelsea Allen

**DESIGNERS**
Abbey Benson
Davis Camp DeLisi
Annie Glover

**JUNIOR DESIGNER**
Lauren Haag

### SHIPPING & LOGISTICS

**LOGISTICS MANAGER**
Lauren Gloyne

**CUSTOMER SUPPORT SPECIALIST**
Katy McKnight

**FULFILLMENT LEAD**
Abigail Achord

**FULFILLMENT SPECIALISTS**
Cait Baggerman
Noe Sanchez

**SUBSCRIPTION INQUIRIES**
orders@hereadstruth.com

**COLOPHON**

This book was printed offset in Nashville, Tennessee, on 60# Lynx Opaque Text under the direction of He Reads Truth. The cover is 100# matte with a soft touch aqueous coating.

HEREADSTRUTH.COM          @HEREADSTRUTH          Download the He Reads Truth app, available for iOS and Android

# COLOSSIANS AND PHILEMON

HE READS TRUTH

The gospel cannot be divorced
from the rest of our lives
because it is our life.

When asked who you are, what do you say? If asked what defines you, what words come to mind?

In the opening chapter of his letter to the Colossians, Paul describes Jesus in six lyrical verses. "He is the image of the invisible God, the firstborn over all creation," Paul says, "...all things have been created through him and for him." Not only that, but "He is before all things, and by him all things hold together." Jesus is both our source and our salvation, reconciling everything to Himself "by making peace through his blood, shed on the cross" (Colossians 1:15-20).

This is our Savior. This is "Christ in [us], the hope of glory" (Colossians 1:27).

As gospel believers, Jesus is the truest, most defining part of us—not our successes or failures, personalities or circumstances, not even our cultures or families. More pervasive than any label the world might give is our identity as children of God who have been saved by grace, justified by faith, and redeemed in love by the One who holds all things together.

In his letter to the church at Colossae, Paul teaches that Christ's identity—and our identity in Him—shapes every part of our lives. It is the unchanging and immovable foundation for our beliefs, our actions, our thoughts, our relationships, and our hope. The gospel cannot be divorced from the rest of our lives because it is our life.

In this study, we're reading Paul's letter to Philemon alongside Colossians. Written around the same time, this tiny letter is a practical application of the gospel Paul proclaims to the Colossians. It gives us a window into how his own life was shaped in unorthodox ways by the freedom, love, and forgiveness of the gospel, and how he expected the same from his brothers and sisters in the faith.

As you get started, take a look at "How to Read a New Testament Letter" on page 12; it has some helpful reminders for engaging this unique literary genre. And when you get to Colossians 1:15-20, take time to dig a little deeper using the cross references provided. Above all, look for Jesus in these pages. When we see Him for who He is, we begin to understand who we really are.

THE HE READS TRUTH TEAM

Each He Reads Truth resource is thoughtfully and artfully designed to highlight the beauty, goodness, and truth of Scripture in a way that reflects the themes of each curated reading plan.

Terrazzo, a composite tile, is created by blending together several different materials—marble, granite, quartz, and glass. This Legacy Book features a terrazzo pattern with red and gold tones, reflecting Paul's message of unity among a diverse group of believers.

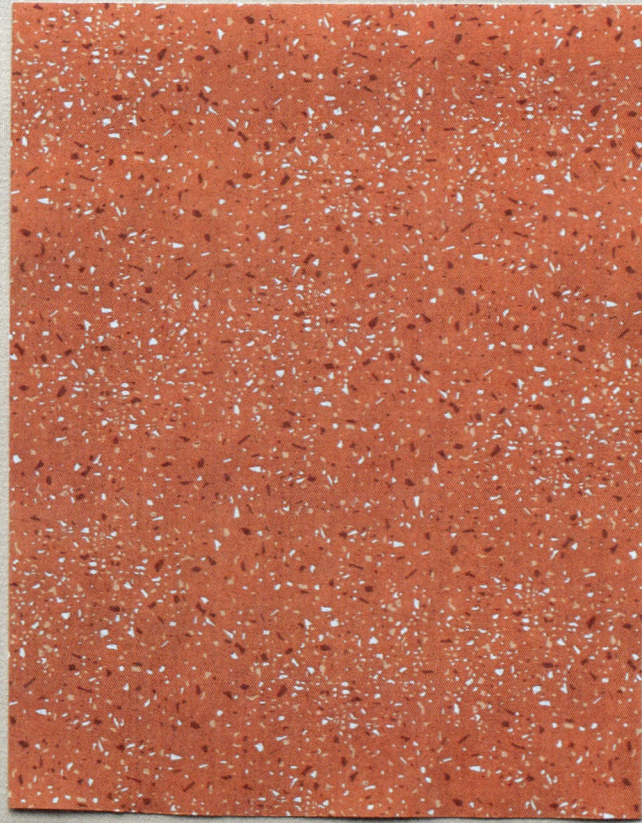

The color red traditionally represents love and is used here as a nod to the love and faith Paul saw in the Christians in Colossae.

# HOW TO USE THIS BOOK

He Reads Truth is a community of men dedicated to reading the Word of God every day. The Bible is living and active, and we confidently hold it higher than anything we can do or say.

## READ & REFLECT

This **Colossians and Philemon** Legacy Book focuses primarily on Scripture, with bonus resources to facilitate deeper engagement with God's Word.

## SCRIPTURE READING

Designed for a Monday start, this Legacy Book presents the books of Colossians and Philemon in daily readings, with supplemental passages for additional context.

## REFLECTION

Each weekday features questions for personal reflection.

## COMMUNITY & CONVERSATION

Join men from across the globe as they open their Bibles every day.

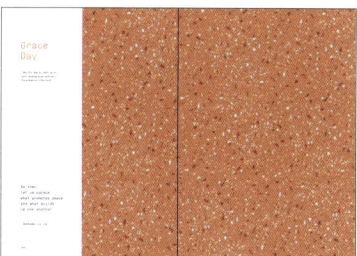

### GRACE DAY

Use Saturdays to catch up on your reading, pray, and rest in the presence of the Lord.

### WEEKLY TRUTH

Sundays are set aside for Scripture memorization.

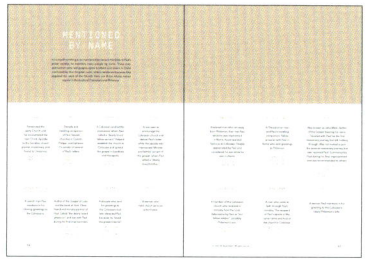

### EXTRAS

This book features additional tools to help you gain a deeper understanding of the text.

*See a complete list of extras on the following page.*

### HE READS TRUTH APP

Devotionals corresponding to each daily reading can be found in the **Colossians and Philemon** reading plan on the He Reads Truth app. You can also participate in community discussions, download free lock screens for Weekly Truth memorization, and more.

### HEREADSTRUTH.COM

All of our reading plans and devotionals are also available at HeReadsTruth.com. Invite your family, friends, and neighbors to read along with you.

# 1

# 2

## EXTRAS

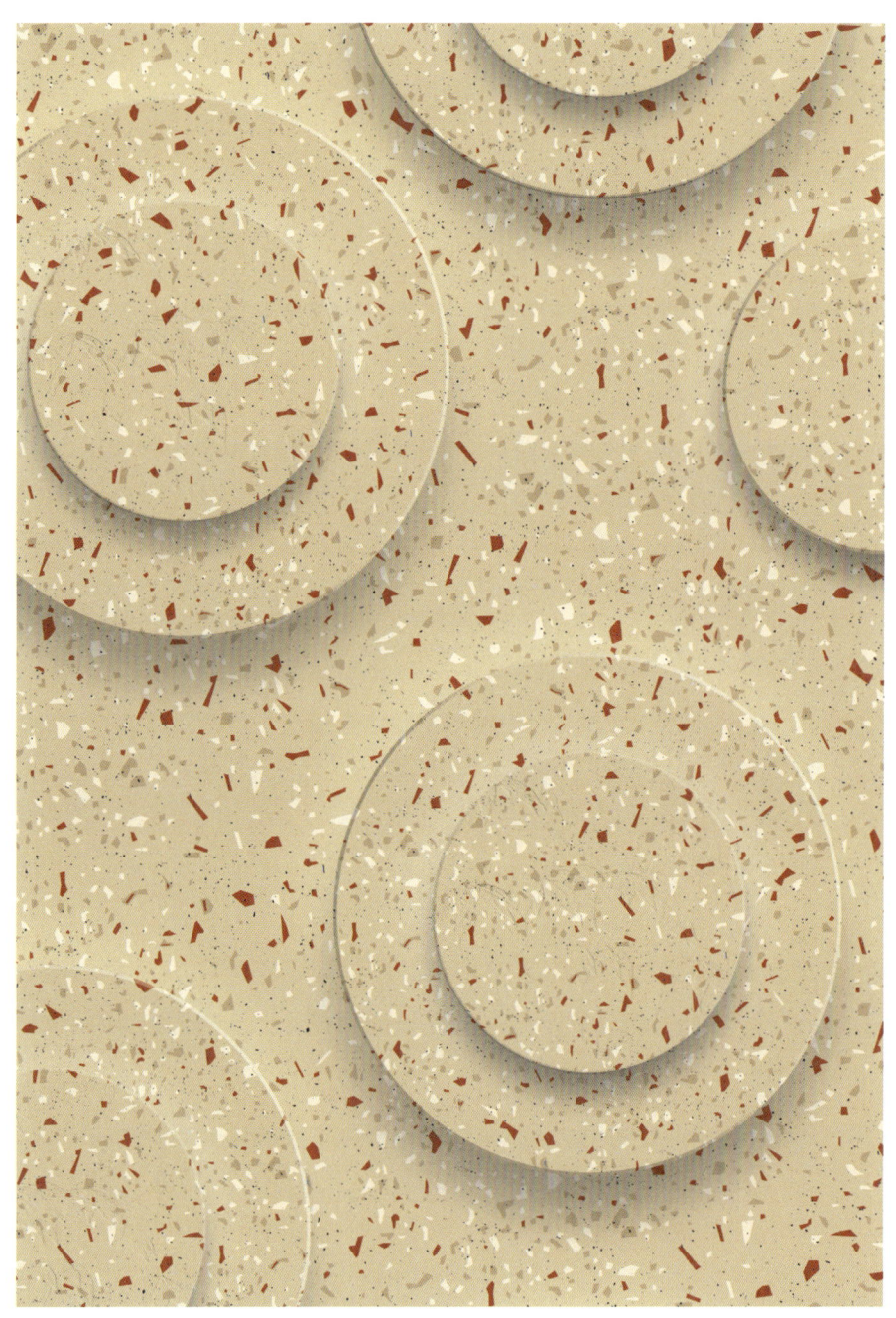

# HOW TO READ A NEW TESTAMENT LETTER

Most of the books that make up the New Testament are letters. These letters, also called *epistles*, come in a variety of shapes and sizes. Many are considered lengthy by ancient standards. Some, like Colossians, were addressed to churches, while others, like Philemon, were written to individuals.

HERE ARE SOME PRINCIPLES TO KEEP IN MIND AS YOU READ COLOSSIANS, PHILEMON, AND OTHER NEW TESTAMENT LETTERS.

| | |
|---|---|
| **READING A LETTER CAN BE LIKE LISTENING TO ONE SIDE OF A CONVERSATION.** | Because we don't always know what specific questions or situations a writer was addressing, we must look for clues in what was written to figure out what was going on. |
| **LETTERS WERE MEANT TO BE READ ALL AT ONCE.** | While there's nothing wrong with studying a particular passage or even a single verse, ancient letters, like the letters we write today, were meant to be read in a single sitting. Doing so allows the reader to see the author's progression of thought and make connections that might otherwise be missed. |
| **THE NEW TESTAMENT LETTERS WERE WRITTEN TO BELIEVERS LEARNING TO LIVE IN CHRISTIAN COMMUNITY.** | With a few exceptions (1 & 2 Timothy, Titus, Philemon, and 3 John), the letters in the New Testament were written to churches—groups of people who were learning to live as the people of God. When you see the word "you" in these letters, it's usually plural. These letters were typically read out loud so all could hear, and they were even shared between congregations (Col 4:16). |

## INSTRUCTIONS WERE OFTEN TAILORED FOR A SPECIFIC AUDIENCE.

Not every instruction is meant to be applied by readers today. Some bits of guidance were written to counter a specific problem or abuse, while others articulate principles that are universally true at all times.

## NEW TESTAMENT LETTERS DRAW HEAVILY ON THE OLD TESTAMENT.

The Old Testament was the Bible of the early Church. Because it was "profitable for teaching, for rebuking, for correcting, [and] for training in righteousness" (2Tm 3:16), it was rightly applied to situations of all kinds. The more we know the Old Testament, the better equipped we will be to understand the New Testament letters.

## THE NEW TESTAMENT LETTERS WERE ALL WRITTEN TO PEOPLE LEARNING TO FOLLOW CHRIST.

Whether Jewish or Gentile believers, the recipients of the New Testament letters had been rescued from the kingdom of darkness (Col 1:13). Nearly everything they thought they knew about the world and their place in it changed as a result of their entrance into God's kingdom. This new life came with its share of spiritual attacks, persecution, and mistakes. We read these letters today as fellow citizens who also have room to grow.

## THE NEW TESTAMENT LETTERS ARE PART OF OUR FAMILY HISTORY.

These letters make up some of the earliest records we have of the Church. Much has changed in the last two thousand years, but the faith that brought hope to Christians in the Greco-Roman world is the same faith we hold on to today. Despite differences in culture, education, and language, we have much in common with the original recipients of the New Testament letters, namely the love of Jesus Christ.

## JESUS IS THE POINT.

Though the New Testament letters were written years after Jesus's life, death, and resurrection, each and every one is about Him. These documents were penned so that readers would grow in their understanding of who He is, what He has done and has promised to do, and, as a result, become more like Him.

## ON THE TIMELINE

Paul wrote Colossians during his first Roman imprisonment (Col 4:3, 10, 18) in the early AD 60s. Together with Ephesians, Philippians, and Philemon, Paul's letter to the Colossians is commonly classified as a prison epistle.

## A LITTLE BACKGROUND

During his ministry in Ephesus (Ac 19:10), Paul sent Epaphras to spread the gospel in the Lycus Valley. Epaphras subsequently established the church at Colossae (Col 1:7; 4:12-13). The city's population consisted mostly of Phrygians and Greeks, but it also included a significant number of Jews. Likewise, the church was composed mostly of Gentiles (Col 1:21, 27; 2:13), but it also had Jewish members (Col 2:11, 16, 18, 21; 3:11). When Epaphras (Phm 23) informed Paul of certain heretical teachings that had spread there, Paul wrote the letter to the Colossians as a theological antidote.

## MESSAGE & PURPOSE

Paul wrote this letter to counter a false teaching in Colossae that was contrary to the gospel of Jesus Christ. The false teaching is identified as a "philosophy" (Col 2:8), presumably drawn from some Hellenistic traditions as indicated by the references to the "fullness" (Col 1:19), the "elements of the world" (Col 2:8), "wisdom" (Col 2:3, 23), and "self-made religion" (Col 2:23).

This false gospel contained several Jewish elements, from circumcision (Col 2:11; 3:11) and "human tradition" (Col 2:8), to Sabbath observance, food regulations, festival participation (Col 2:16), and more. Paul addressed this combination of philosophies by teaching a proper understanding of the gospel of Jesus Christ and its appropriate implications for Christian salvation (Col 2:10, 13, 20; 3:1, 11-12, 17) and conduct (Col 3:5-4:6).

## GIVE THANKS FOR THE BOOK OF COLOSSIANS

Colossians provides one of the Bible's fullest expressions of the deity and supremacy of Christ. This is most evident in the magnificent hymn of praise found in Colossians 1:15-20, which sets forth Christ as the image of the invisible God, the Creator and sustainer of the universe. He is the head of His body, the Church, and the One through whom forgiveness is possible.

# Paul's Letter to the Colossians

The book of Colossians is a letter, originally intended to be read all at once. Take some time before you begin Day 1 to read the letter in one sitting, tracing the themes throughout before engaging with each individual chapter.

PAUL, AN APOSTLE OF CHRIST JESUS BY GOD'S WILL, AND TIMOTHY OUR BROTHER:

To the saints in Christ at Colossae, who are faithful brothers and sisters.

Grace to you and peace from God our Father.

We always thank God, the Father of our Lord Jesus Christ, when we pray for you, for we have heard of your faith in Christ Jesus and of the love you have for all the saints because of the hope reserved for you in heaven. You have already heard about this hope in the word of truth, the gospel that has come to you. It is bearing fruit and growing all over the world, just as it has among you since the day you heard it and came to truly appreciate God's grace. You learned this from Epaphras, our dearly loved fellow servant. He is a faithful minister of Christ on your behalf, and he has told us about your love in the Spirit.

For this reason also, since the day we heard this, we haven't stopped praying for you. We are asking that you may be filled with the knowledge of his will in all wisdom and spiritual understanding, so that you may walk worthy of the Lord, fully pleasing to him: bearing fruit in every good work and growing in the knowledge of God, being strengthened with all power, according to his glorious might, so that you may have great endurance and patience, joyfully giving thanks to the Father, who has enabled you to share in the saints' inheritance in the light. He has rescued us from the domain of darkness and transferred us into the kingdom of the Son he loves. In him we have redemption, the forgiveness of sins.

He is the image of the invisible God,
the firstborn over all creation.
For everything was created by him,
in heaven and on earth,
the visible and the invisible,
whether thrones or dominions
or rulers or authorities—
all things have been created through him and for him.
He is before all things,
and by him all things hold together.
He is also the head of the body, the church;
he is the beginning,
the firstborn from the dead,
so that he might come to have
first place in everything.

For God was pleased to have
all his fullness dwell in him,
and through him to reconcile
everything to himself,
whether things on earth or things in heaven,
by making peace
through his blood, shed on the cross.

Once you were alienated and hostile in your minds as expressed in your evil actions. But now he has reconciled you by his physical body through his death, to present you holy, faultless, and blameless before him—if indeed you remain grounded and steadfast in the faith and are not shifted away from the hope of the gospel that you heard. This gospel has been proclaimed in all creation under heaven, and I, Paul, have become a servant of it.

Now I rejoice in my sufferings for you, and I am completing in my flesh what is lacking in Christ's afflictions for his body, that is, the church. I have become its servant, according to God's commission that was given to me for you, to make the word of God fully known, the mystery hidden for ages and generations but now revealed to his saints. God wanted to make known among the Gentiles the glorious wealth of this mystery, which is Christ in you, the hope of glory. We proclaim him, warning and teaching everyone with all wisdom, so that we may present everyone mature in Christ. I labor for this, striving with his strength that works powerfully in me.

For I want you to know how greatly I am struggling for you, for those in Laodicea, and for all who have not seen me in person. I want their hearts to be encouraged and joined together in love, so that they may have all the riches of complete understanding and have the knowledge of God's mystery—Christ. In him are hidden all the treasures of wisdom and knowledge.

I am saying this so that no one will deceive you with arguments that sound reasonable. For I may be absent in body, but I am with you in spirit, rejoicing to see how well ordered you are and the strength of your faith in Christ.

So then, just as you have received Christ Jesus as Lord, continue to walk in him, being rooted and built up in him and established in the faith, just as you were taught, and overflowing with gratitude.

Be careful that no one takes you captive through philosophy and empty deceit based on human tradition, based on the elements of the world, rather than

Christ. For the entire fullness of God's nature dwells bodily in Christ, and you have been filled by him, who is the head over every ruler and authority. You were also circumcised in him with a circumcision not done with hands, by putting off the body of flesh, in the circumcision of Christ, when you were buried with him in baptism, in which you were also raised with him through faith in the working of God, who raised him from the dead. And when you were dead in trespasses and in the uncircumcision of your flesh, he made you alive with him and forgave us all our trespasses. He erased the certificate of debt, with its obligations, that was against us and opposed to us, and has taken it away by nailing it to the cross. He disarmed the rulers and authorities and disgraced them publicly; he triumphed over them in him.

Therefore, don't let anyone judge you in regard to food and drink or in the matter of a festival or a new moon or a Sabbath day. These are a shadow of what was to come; the substance is Christ. Let no one condemn you by delighting in ascetic practices and the worship of angels, claiming access to a visionary realm. Such people are inflated by empty notions of their unspiritual mind. He doesn't hold on to the head, from whom the whole body, nourished and held together by its ligaments and tendons, grows with growth from God.

If you died with Christ to the elements of this world, why do you live as if you still belonged to the world? Why do you submit to regulations: "Don't handle, don't taste, don't touch"? All these regulations refer to what is destined to perish by being used up; they are human commands and doctrines. Although these have a reputation for wisdom by promoting self-made religion, false humility, and severe treatment of the body, they are not of any value in curbing self-indulgence.

So if you have been raised with Christ, seek the things above, where Christ is, seated at the right hand of God. Set your minds on things above, not on earthly things. For you died, and your life is hidden with Christ in God. When Christ, who is your life, appears, then you also will appear with him in glory.

Therefore, put to death what belongs to your earthly nature: sexual immorality, impurity, lust, evil desire, and greed, which is idolatry. Because of these, God's wrath is coming upon the disobedient, and you once walked in these things when you were living in them. But now, put away all the following: anger, wrath, malice, slander, and filthy language from your mouth. Do not lie to one another, since you have put off the old self with its practices and have put on the new self. You are being renewed in knowledge according to the image of your Creator. In Christ there is not Greek and Jew, circumcision and uncircumcision, barbarian, Scythian, slave and free; but Christ is all and in all.

Therefore, as God's chosen ones, holy and dearly loved, put on compassion, kindness, humility, gentleness, and patience, bearing with one another and forgiving one another if anyone has a grievance against another. Just as the Lord has forgiven you, so you are also to forgive. Above all, put on love, which is the perfect bond of unity. And let the peace of Christ, to which you were also called in one body, rule your hearts. And be thankful. Let the word of Christ dwell richly among you, in all wisdom teaching and admonishing one another through psalms, hymns, and spiritual songs, singing to God with gratitude in your hearts. And whatever you do, in word or in deed, do everything in the name of the Lord Jesus, giving thanks to God the Father through him.

Wives, submit yourselves to your husbands, as is fitting in the Lord. Husbands, love your wives and don't be bitter toward them. Children, obey your parents in everything, for this pleases the Lord. Fathers, do not exasperate your children, so that they won't become discouraged. Slaves, obey your human masters in everything. Don't work only while being watched, as people-pleasers, but work wholeheartedly, fearing the Lord. Whatever you do, do it from the heart, as something done for the Lord and not for people, knowing that you will receive the reward of an inheritance from the Lord. You serve the Lord Christ. For the wrongdoer will be paid back for whatever wrong he has done, and there is no favoritism.

Masters, deal with your slaves justly and fairly, since you know that you too have a Master in heaven.

Devote yourselves to prayer; stay alert in it with thanksgiving. At the same time, pray also for us that God may open a door to us for the word, to speak the mystery of Christ, for which I am in chains, so that I may make it known as I should. Act wisely toward outsiders, making the most of the time. Let your speech always be gracious, seasoned with salt, so that you may know how you should answer each person.

Tychicus, our dearly loved brother, faithful minister, and fellow servant in the Lord, will tell you all the news about me. I have sent him to you for this very purpose, so that you may know how we are and so that he may encourage your hearts. He is coming with Onesimus, a faithful and dearly loved brother, who is one of you. They will tell you about everything here.

Aristarchus, my fellow prisoner, sends you greetings, as does Mark, Barnabas's cousin (concerning whom you have received instructions: if he comes to you, welcome him), and so does Jesus who is called Justus. These alone of the circumcised are my coworkers for the kingdom of God, and they have been a comfort to me. Epaphras, who is one of you, a servant of Christ Jesus, sends you greetings. He is always wrestling for you in his prayers, so that you can stand mature and fully assured in everything God wills. For I testify about him that he works hard for you, for those in Laodicea, and for those in Hierapolis. Luke, the dearly loved physician, and Demas send you greetings. Give my greetings to the brothers and sisters in Laodicea, and to Nympha and the church in her home. After this letter has been read at your gathering, have it read also in the church of the Laodiceans; and see that you also read the letter from Laodicea. And tell Archippus, "Pay attention to the ministry you have received in the Lord, so that you can accomplish it."

I, Paul, am writing this greeting with my own hand. Remember my chains. Grace be with you.

# Paul's Letter to Philemon

Like Colossians, the book of Philemon is also a letter. Take some time before you begin Day 11 to read Philemon in one sitting, tracing the themes throughout before engaging with each individual verse.

To Philemon our dear friend and coworker, to Apphia our sister, to Archippus our fellow soldier, and to the church that meets in your home.

Grace to you and peace from God our Father and the Lord Jesus Christ.

I always thank my God when I mention you in my prayers, because I hear of your love for all the saints and the faith that you have in the Lord Jesus. I pray that your participation in the faith may become effective through knowing every good thing that is in us for the glory of Christ. For I have great joy and encouragement from your love, because the hearts of the saints have been refreshed through you, brother.

For this reason, although I have great boldness in Christ to command you to do what is right, I appeal to you, instead, on the basis of love. I, Paul, as an elderly man and now also as a prisoner of Christ Jesus, appeal to you for my son, Onesimus. I became his father while I was in chains. Once he was useless to you, but now he is useful both to you and to me. I am sending him back to you—I am sending my very own heart. I wanted to keep him with me, so that in my imprisonment for the gospel he might serve me in your place. But I didn't want to do anything without your consent, so that your good deed might not be out of obligation, but of your own free will. For perhaps this is why he was separated from you for a brief time, so that you might get him back permanently, no longer as a slave, but more than a slave—as a dearly loved brother. He is especially so to me, but how much more to you, both in the flesh and in the Lord.

So if you consider me a partner, welcome him as you would me. And if he has wronged you in any way, or owes you anything, charge that to my account. I, Paul, write this with my own hand: I will repay it—not to mention to you that you owe me even your very self. Yes, brother, may I benefit from you in the Lord; refresh my heart in Christ. Since I am confident of your obedience, I am writing to you, knowing that you will do even more than I say. Meanwhile, also prepare a guest room for me, since I hope that through your prayers I will be restored to you.

Epaphras, my fellow prisoner in Christ Jesus, sends you greetings, and so do Mark, Aristarchus, Demas, and Luke, my coworkers.

The grace of the Lord Jesus Christ be with your spirit.

# Thanksgiving

## COLOSSIANS 1:1-14

### GREETING

[1] Paul, an apostle of Christ Jesus by God's will, and Timothy our brother:

[2] To the saints in Christ at Colossae, who are faithful brothers and sisters.

Grace to you and peace from God our Father.

### THANKSGIVING

[3] We always thank God, the Father of our Lord Jesus Christ, when we pray for you, [4] for we have heard of your faith in Christ Jesus and of the love you have for all the saints [5] because of the hope reserved for you in heaven. You have already heard about this hope in the word of truth, the gospel [6] that has come to you. It is bearing fruit and growing all over the world, just as it has among you since the day you heard it and came to truly appreciate God's grace. [7] You learned this from Epaphras, our dearly loved fellow servant. He is a faithful minister of Christ on your behalf, [8] and he has told us about your love in the Spirit.

⁹ For this reason also, since the day we heard this, we haven't stopped praying for you. We are asking that you may be filled with the knowledge of his will in all wisdom and spiritual understanding, ¹⁰ so that you may walk worthy of the Lord, fully pleasing to him: bearing fruit in every good work and growing in the knowledge of God, ¹¹ being strengthened with all power, according to his glorious might, so that you may have great endurance and patience, joyfully ¹² giving thanks to the Father, who has enabled you to share in the saints' inheritance in the light. ¹³ He has rescued us from the domain of darkness and transferred us into the kingdom of the Son he loves. ¹⁴ In him we have redemption, the forgiveness of sins.

## PSALM 1:1–3

THE TWO WAYS

¹ How happy is the one who does not
walk in the advice of the wicked
or stand in the pathway with sinners
or sit in the company of mockers!
² Instead, his delight is in the LORD's instruction,
and he meditates on it day and night.
³ He is like a tree planted beside flowing streams
that bears its fruit in its season,
and its leaf does not wither.
Whatever he does prospers.

## MATTHEW 24:14

"This good news of the kingdom will be proclaimed in all the world as a testimony to all nations, and then the end will come."

## 1 JOHN 3:1–2

¹ See what great love the Father has given us that we should be called God's children—and we are! The reason the world does not know us is that it didn't know him. ² Dear friends, we are God's children now, and what we will be has not yet been revealed. We know that when he appears, we will be like him because we will see him as he is.

## QUESTIONS

1 . Summarize Colossians 1:1-14 in one or two sentences.
What did you observe in today's reading?

2 . How does today's reading convict you?
How does it encourage you?

3 . Paul wrote Colossians, in part, to correct false teaching.
How does today's reading from Colossians correct or
clarify your understanding of the gospel?

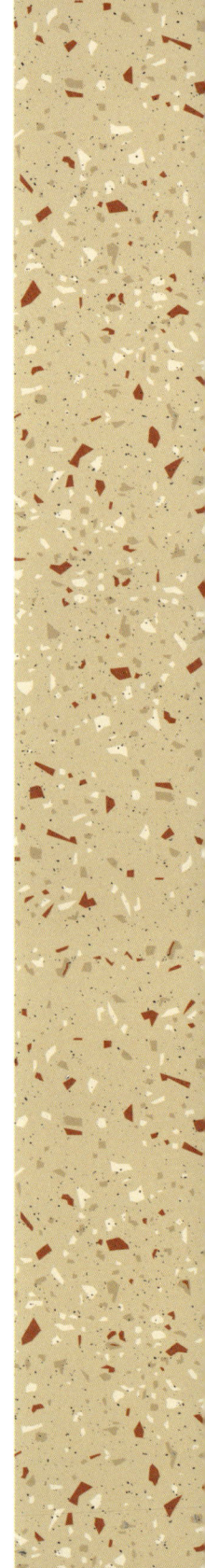

# The Centrality of Christ

## COLOSSIANS 1:15–23

### THE CENTRALITY OF CHRIST

Colossians contains some of the Bible's most robust expressions of the deity and supremacy of Christ. Passages like this one also include allusions and parallels connecting the Old and New Testaments. Shown here are some cross references between this passage of praise and other scriptures.

Psalm 89:27
Hebrews 1:6

Nehemiah 9:6
John 1:3, 10
Romans 11:36
1 Corinthians 8:6
Hebrews 1:2

John 8:58

Acts 26:23
Romans 8:29
1 Corinthians 15:20
Ephesians 1:22–23
Revelation 1:5

John 1:16
Colossians 2:9

Romans 5:1
2 Corinthians 5:18
Ephesians 2:14

[15] He is the image of the invisible God,
the firstborn over all creation.
[16] For everything was created by him,
in heaven and on earth,
the visible and the invisible,
whether thrones or dominions
or rulers or authorities—
all things have been created through him and for him.
[17] He is before all things,
and by him all things hold together.
[18] He is also the head of the body, the church;
he is the beginning,
the firstborn from the dead,
so that he might come to have
first place in everything.
[19] For God was pleased to have
all his fullness dwell in him,
[20] and through him to reconcile
everything to himself,
whether things on earth or things in heaven,
by making peace
through his blood, shed on the cross.

John 1:1, 18
2 Corinthians 4:4
Philippians 2:6
Hebrews 1:3

21 Once you were alienated and hostile in your minds as expressed in your evil actions.

22 But now he has reconciled you by his physical body through his death, to present you holy, faultless, and blameless before him—

23 if indeed you remain grounded and steadfast in the faith and are not shifted away from the hope of the gospel that you heard. This gospel has been proclaimed in all creation under heaven, and I, Paul, have become a servant of it.

## GENESIS 1:1, 26-27

THE CREATION

1 In the beginning God created the heavens and the earth.

…

26 Then God said, "Let us make man in our image, according to our likeness. They will rule the fish of the sea, the birds of the sky, the livestock, the whole earth, and the creatures that crawl on the earth."

27 So God created man
in his own image;
he created him in the image of God;
he created them male and female.

## 1 CORINTHIANS 8:5-6

5 For even if there are so-called gods, whether in heaven or on earth—as there are many "gods" and many "lords"— 6 yet for us there is one God, the Father. All things are from him, and we exist for him. And there is one Lord, Jesus Christ. All things are through him, and we exist through him.

### JUDE 24-25

[24] Now to him who is able to protect you from stumbling and to make you stand in the presence of his glory, without blemish and with great joy, [25] to the only God our Savior, through Jesus Christ our Lord, be glory, majesty, power, and authority before all time, now and forever. Amen.

1 . Summarize Colossians 1:15-23 in one or two
sentences. What did you observe in today's reading?

2 . How does today's reading convict you?
How does it encourage you?

3 . How does today's reading from Colossians correct or
clarify your understanding of the gospel?

# Christ, the Hope of Glory

## COLOSSIANS 1:24-29

### PAUL'S MINISTRY

24 Now I rejoice in my sufferings for you, and I am completing in my flesh what is lacking in Christ's afflictions for his body, that is, the church. 25 I have become its servant, according to God's commission that was given to me for you, to make the word of God fully known, 26 the mystery hidden for ages and generations but now revealed to his saints. 27 God wanted to make known among the Gentiles the glorious wealth of this mystery, which is Christ in you, the hope of glory. 28 We proclaim him, warning and teaching everyone with all wisdom, so that we may present everyone mature in Christ. 29 I labor for this, striving with his strength that works powerfully in me.

## COLOSSIANS 2:1-7

1 For I want you to know how greatly I am struggling for you, for those in Laodicea, and for all who have not seen me in person. 2 I want their hearts to be encouraged and joined together in love, so that they may have all the riches of complete understanding and have the knowledge of God's mystery—Christ. 3 In him are hidden all the treasures of wisdom and knowledge.

### CHRIST VERSUS THE COLOSSIAN HERESY

4 I am saying this so that no one will deceive you with arguments that sound reasonable. 5 For I may be absent in body, but I am with you in spirit, rejoicing to see how well ordered you are and the strength of your faith in Christ.

[6] So then, just as you have received Christ Jesus as Lord, continue to walk in him, [7] being rooted and built up in him and established in the faith, just as you were taught, and overflowing with gratitude.

### ISAIAH 11:1–5

REIGN OF THE DAVIDIC KING

[1] Then a shoot will grow from the stump of Jesse,
and a branch from his roots will bear fruit.
[2] The Spirit of the LORD will rest on him—
a Spirit of wisdom and understanding,
a Spirit of counsel and strength,
a Spirit of knowledge and of the fear of the LORD.
[3] His delight will be in the fear of the LORD.
He will not judge
by what he sees with his eyes,
he will not execute justice
by what he hears with his ears,
[4] but he will judge the poor righteously
and execute justice for the oppressed of the land.
He will strike the land
with a scepter from his mouth,
and he will kill the wicked
with a command from his lips.
[5] Righteousness will be a belt around his hips;
faithfulness will be a belt around his waist.

### 2 TIMOTHY 1:8–10

NOT ASHAMED OF THE GOSPEL

[8] So don't be ashamed of the testimony about our Lord, or of me his prisoner. Instead, share in suffering for the gospel, relying on the power of God. [9] He has saved us and called us with a holy calling, not according to our works, but according to his own purpose and grace, which was given to us in Christ Jesus before time began. [10] This has now been made evident through the appearing of our Savior Christ Jesus, who has abolished death and has brought life and immortality to light through the gospel.

## QUESTIONS

1 . Summarize Colossians 1:24–29 and 2:1-7 in one or two
sentences. What did you observe in today's reading?

2 . How does today's reading convict you?
How does it encourage you?

3 . How does today's reading from Colossians correct or
clarify your understanding of the gospel?

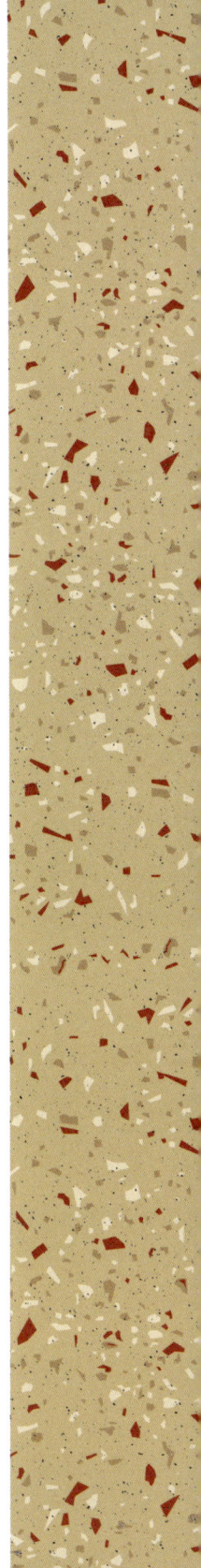

# The True Gospel

## COLOSSIANS 2:8-15

[8] Be careful that no one takes you captive through philosophy and empty deceit based on human tradition, based on the elements of the world, rather than Christ. [9] For the entire fullness of God's nature dwells bodily in Christ, [10] and you have been filled by him, who is the head over every ruler and authority. [11] You were also circumcised in him with a circumcision not done with hands, by putting off the body of flesh, in the circumcision of Christ, [12] when you were buried with him in baptism, in which you were also raised with him through faith in the working of God, who raised him from the dead. [13] And when you were dead in trespasses and in the uncircumcision of your flesh, he made you alive with him and forgave us all our trespasses. [14] He erased the certificate of debt, with its obligations, that was against us and opposed to us, and has taken it away by nailing it to the cross. [15] He disarmed the rulers and authorities and disgraced them publicly; he triumphed over them in him.

### DEUTERONOMY 10:16–17

[16] Therefore, circumcise your hearts and don't be stiff-necked any longer.

[17] For the LORD your God is the God of gods and Lord of lords,

the great, mighty, and awe-inspiring God, showing no partiality and taking no bribe.

### MATTHEW 15:1–9

THE TRADITION OF THE ELDERS

[1] Then Jesus was approached by Pharisees and scribes from Jerusalem, who asked, [2] "Why do your disciples break the tradition of the elders? For they don't wash their hands when they eat."

[3] He answered them, "Why do you break God's commandment because of your tradition? [4] For God said: Honor your father and your mother; and, Whoever speaks evil of father or mother must be put to death. [5] But you say, 'Whoever tells his father or mother, "Whatever benefit you might have received from me is a gift committed to the temple," [6] he does not have to honor his father.' In this way, you have nullified the word of God because of your tradition. [7] Hypocrites! Isaiah prophesied correctly about you when he said:

[8] This people honors me with their lips,
but their heart is far from me.
[9] They worship me in vain,
teaching as doctrines human commands."

### MATTHEW 28:5–6

[5] The angel told the women, "Don't be afraid, because I know you are looking for Jesus who was crucified. [6] He is not here. For he has risen, just as he said. Come and see the place where he lay."

## QUESTIONS

1. Summarize Colossians 2:8–15 in one or two sentences.
   What did you observe in today's reading?

2. How does today's reading convict you?
   How does it encourage you?

3. How does today's reading from Colossians correct or
   clarify your understanding of the gospel?

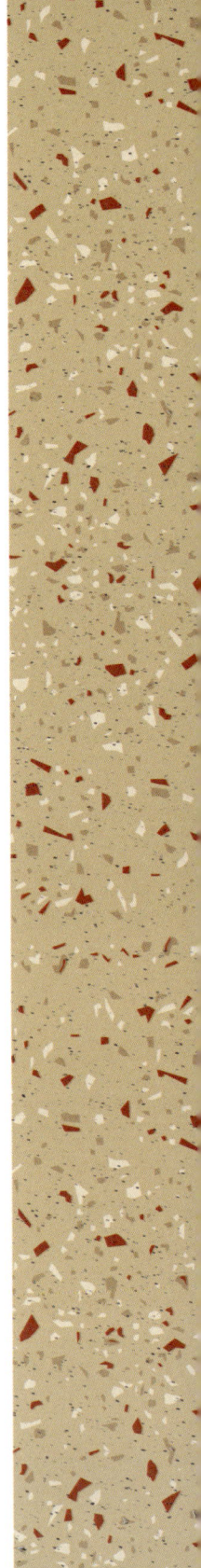

# Warning Against False Teaching

## COLOSSIANS 2:16-23

[16] Therefore, don't let anyone judge you in regard to food and drink or in the matter of a festival or a new moon or a Sabbath day. [17] These are a shadow of what was to come; the substance is Christ. [18] Let no one condemn you by delighting in ascetic practices and the worship of angels, claiming access to a visionary realm. Such people are inflated by empty notions of their unspiritual mind. [19] He doesn't hold on to the head, from whom the whole body, nourished and held together by its ligaments and tendons, grows with growth from God.

[20] If you died with Christ to the elements of this world, why do you live as if you still belonged to the world? Why do you submit to regulations: [21] "Don't handle, don't taste, don't touch"? [22] All these regulations refer to what is destined to perish by being used up; they are human commands and doctrines. [23] Although these have a reputation for wisdom by promoting self-made religion, false humility, and severe treatment of the body, they are not of any value in curbing self-indulgence.

## THE LAW OF LIBERTY

[1] Welcome anyone who is weak in faith, but don't argue about disputed matters. [2] One person believes he may eat anything, while one who is weak eats only vegetables. [3] One who eats must not look down on one who does not eat, and one who does not eat must not judge one who does, because God has accepted him. [4] Who are you to judge another's household servant? Before his own Lord he stands or falls. And he will stand, because the Lord is able to make him stand.

[5] One person judges one day to be more important than another day. Someone else judges every day to be the same. Let each one be fully convinced in his own mind. [6] Whoever observes the day, observes it for the honor of the Lord. Whoever eats, eats for the Lord, since he gives thanks to God; and whoever does not eat, it is for the Lord that he does not eat it, and he gives thanks to God. [7] For none of us lives for himself, and no one dies for himself. [8] If we live, we live for the Lord; and if we die, we die for the Lord. Therefore, whether we live or die, we belong to the Lord. [9] Christ died and returned to life for this: that he might be Lord over both the dead and the living. [10] But you, why do you judge your brother or sister? Or you, why do you despise your brother or sister? For we will all stand before the judgment seat of God. [11] For it is written,

As I live, says the Lord,
every knee will bow to me,
and every tongue will give praise to God.

[12] So then, each of us will give an account of himself to God.

## THE LAW OF LOVE

[13] Therefore, let us no longer judge one another. Instead decide never to put a stumbling block or pitfall in the way of your brother or sister. [14] I know and am persuaded in the Lord Jesus that nothing is unclean in itself. Still, to someone who considers a thing to be unclean, to that one it is unclean. [15] For if your brother or sister is hurt by what you eat, you are no longer walking according to love. Do not destroy, by what you eat, someone for whom Christ died. [16] Therefore, do not let your good be slandered, [17] for the kingdom of God is not eating and drinking, but righteousness, peace, and joy in the Holy Spirit. [18] Whoever serves Christ in this way is acceptable to God and receives human approval.

[19] So then,

## let us pursue what promotes peace and what builds up one another.

[20] Do not tear down God's work because of food. Everything is clean, but it is wrong to make someone fall by what he eats. [21] It is a good thing not to eat meat, or drink wine, or do anything that makes your brother or sister stumble. [22] Whatever you believe about these things, keep between yourself and God. Blessed is the one who does not condemn himself by what he approves. [23] But whoever doubts stands condemned if he eats, because his eating is not from faith, and everything that is not from faith is sin.

### JAMES 3:13–18

THE WISDOM FROM ABOVE

[13] Who among you is wise and understanding? By his good conduct he should show that his works are done in the gentleness that comes from wisdom. [14] But if you have bitter envy and selfish ambition in your heart, don't boast and deny the truth. [15] Such wisdom does not come down from above but is earthly, unspiritual, demonic. [16] For where there is envy and selfish ambition, there is disorder and every evil practice. [17] But the wisdom from above is first pure, then peace-loving, gentle, compliant, full of mercy and good fruits, unwavering, without pretense. [18] And the fruit of righteousness is sown in peace by those who cultivate peace.

1 . Summarize Colossians 2:16–23 in one or two
sentences. What did you observe in today's reading?

2 . How does today's reading convict you?
How does it encourage you?

3 . How does today's reading from Colossians correct or
clarify your understanding of the gospel?

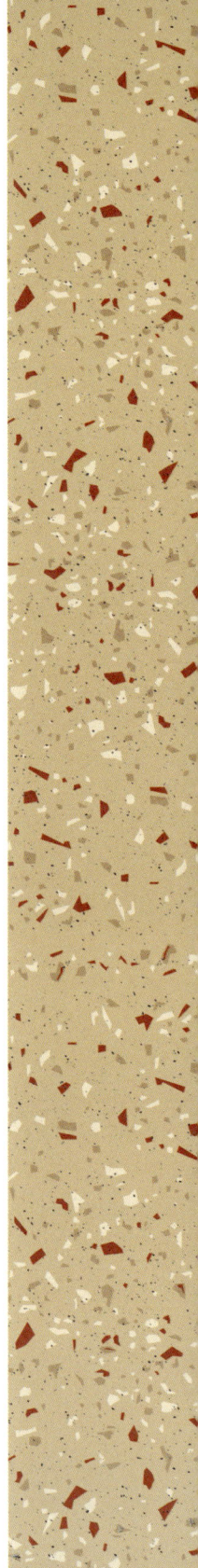

# Grace
# Day

Take this day to catch up on
your reading, pray, and rest in
the presence of the Lord.

So then,
let us pursue
what promotes peace
and what builds
up one another.

ROMANS 14:19

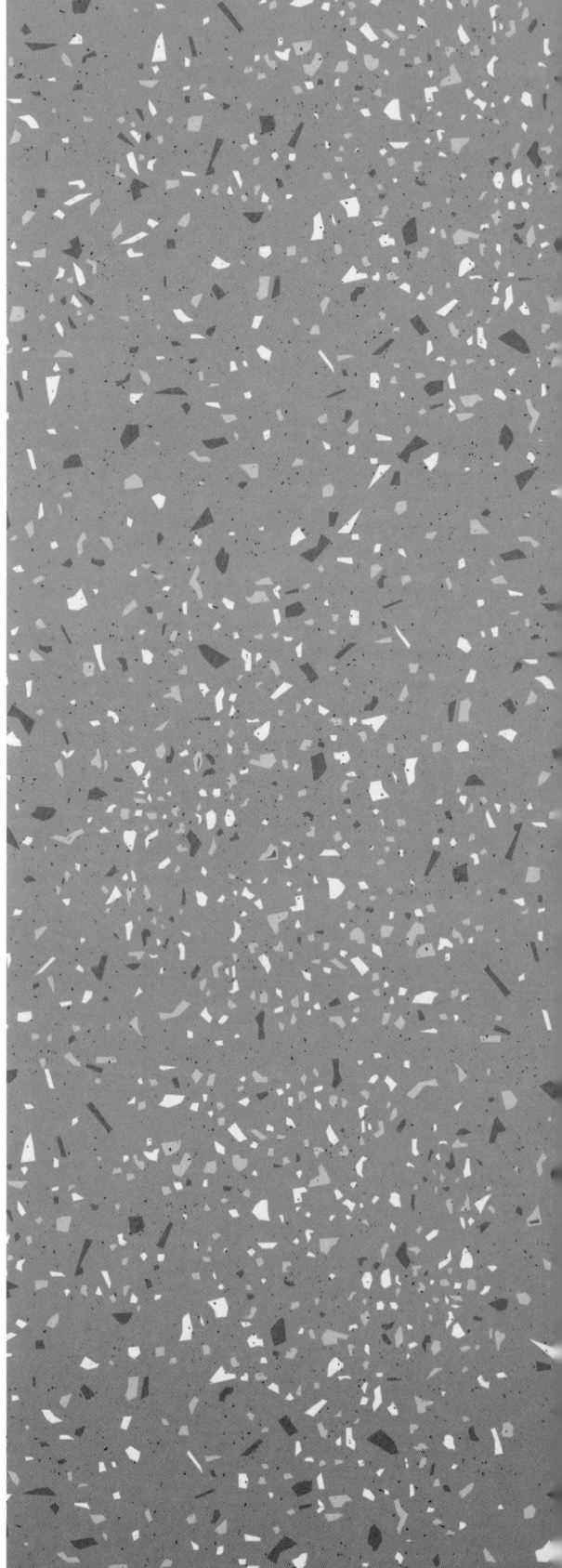

He is before all
things, and by him all
things hold together.

COLOSSIANS 1:17

# Weekly Truth

Scripture is God-breathed and true. When we memorize it, we carry the good news of Jesus with us wherever we go.

This week, let's memorize this key verse from the book of Colossians about Jesus's dominion over creation. Write the verse on a note card or separate piece of paper, then go back and underline key words. Meditate on what it means that Christ holds all things together, both in your personal life and in the world.

# New Life in Christ

## COLOSSIANS 3:1-17

### THE LIFE OF THE NEW MAN

[1] So if you have been raised with Christ, seek the things above, where Christ is, seated at the right hand of God. [2] Set your minds on things above, not on earthly things. [3] For you died, and your life is hidden with Christ in God. [4] When Christ, who is your life, appears, then you also will appear with him in glory.

[5] Therefore, put to death what belongs to your earthly nature: sexual immorality, impurity, lust, evil desire, and greed, which is idolatry. [6] Because of these, God's wrath is coming upon the disobedient, [7] and you once walked in these things when you were living in them. [8] But now, put away all the following: anger, wrath, malice, slander, and filthy language from your mouth. [9] Do not lie to one another, since you have put off the old self with its practices [10] and have put on the new self. You are being renewed in knowledge according to the image of your Creator. [11] In Christ there is not Greek and Jew, circumcision and uncircumcision, barbarian, Scythian, slave and free; but Christ is all and in all.

[12] Therefore, as God's chosen ones, holy and dearly loved, put on compassion, kindness, humility, gentleness, and patience, [13] bearing with one another and forgiving one another if anyone has a grievance against another. Just as the Lord has forgiven you, so you are also to forgive.

[14] **Above all, put on love, which is the perfect bond of unity.**

[15] And let the peace of Christ, to which you were also called in one body, rule your hearts. And be thankful. [16] Let the word of Christ dwell richly among you, in all wisdom teaching and admonishing one another through psalms, hymns, and spiritual songs, singing to God with gratitude in your hearts. [17] And whatever you do, in word or in deed, do everything in the name of the Lord Jesus, giving thanks to God the Father through him.

## MATTHEW 6:33

"But seek first the kingdom of God and his righteousness, and all these things will be provided for you."

## JOHN 11:25

Jesus said to her, "I am the resurrection and the life. The one who believes in me, even if he dies, will live."

## ROMANS 6:1–14

### THE NEW LIFE IN CHRIST

[1] What should we say then? Should we continue in sin so that grace may multiply? [2] Absolutely not! How can we who died to sin still live in it?

[3] Or are you unaware that all of us who were baptized into Christ Jesus were baptized into his death? [4] Therefore we were buried with him by baptism into death, in order that, just as Christ was raised from the dead by the glory of the Father, so we too may walk in newness of life. [5] For if we have been united with him in the likeness of his death, we will certainly also be in the likeness of his resurrection. [6] For we know that our old self was crucified with him so that the body ruled by sin might be rendered powerless so that we may no longer be enslaved to sin, [7] since a person who has died is freed from sin. [8] Now if we died with Christ, we believe that we will also live with him, [9] because we know that Christ, having been raised from the dead, will not die again. Death no longer rules over him. [10] For the death he died, he died to sin once for all time; but the life he lives, he lives to God. [11] So, you too consider yourselves dead to sin and alive to God in Christ Jesus.

[12] Therefore do not let sin reign in your mortal body, so that you obey its desires. [13] And do not offer any parts of it to sin as weapons for unrighteousness. But as those who are alive from the dead, offer yourselves to God, and all the parts of yourselves to God as weapons for righteousness. [14] For sin will not rule over you, because you are not under the law but under grace.

1. Summarize Colossians 3:1–17 in one or two sentences.
   What did you observe in today's reading?

2. How does today's reading convict you?
   How does it encourage you?

3. How does today's reading from Colossians correct or
   clarify your understanding of the gospel?

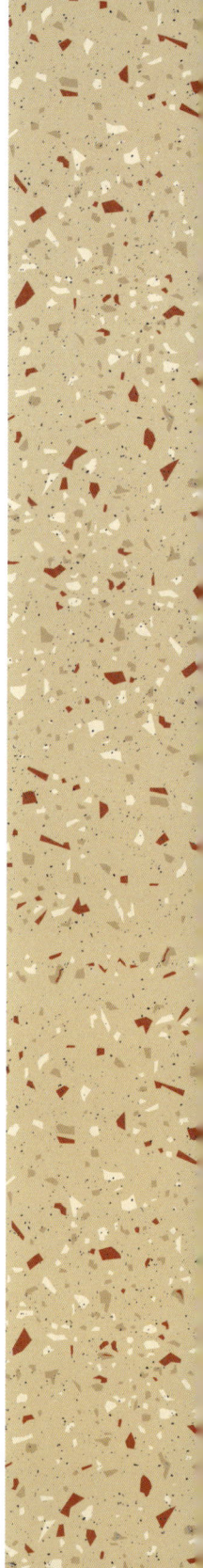

# Christian Living

## COLOSSIANS 3:18-25

### CHRIST IN YOUR HOME

[18] Wives, submit yourselves to your husbands, as is fitting in the Lord.
[19] Husbands, love your wives and don't be bitter toward them. [20] Children,
obey your parents in everything, for this pleases the Lord. [21] Fathers, do
not exasperate your children, so that they won't become discouraged.
[22] Slaves, obey your human masters in everything. Don't work only while
being watched, as people-pleasers, but work wholeheartedly, fearing the
Lord. [23] Whatever you do, do it from the heart, as something done for
the Lord and not for people, [24] knowing that you will receive the reward
of an inheritance from the Lord. You serve the Lord Christ. [25] For the
wrongdoer will be paid back for whatever wrong he has done, and there
is no favoritism.

## COLOSSIANS 4:1

Masters, deal with your slaves justly and fairly, since you know that you
too have a Master in heaven.

⁴ Listen, Israel: The Lᴏʀᴅ our God, the Lᴏʀᴅ is one.

⁵ Love the LORD your God with all your heart, with all your soul, and with all your strength.

## MICAH 6:8

Mankind, he has told each of you what is good
and what it is the Lᴏʀᴅ requires of you:
to act justly,
to love faithfulness,
and to walk humbly with your God.

## EPHESIANS 5:22-33

### WIVES AND HUSBANDS

²² Wives, submit to your husbands as to the Lord, ²³ because the husband is the head of the wife as Christ is the head of the church. He is the Savior of the body. ²⁴ Now as the church submits to Christ, so also wives are to submit to their husbands in everything. ²⁵ Husbands, love your wives, just as Christ loved the church and gave himself for her ²⁶ to make her holy, cleansing her with the washing of water by the word. ²⁷ He did this to present the church to himself in splendor, without spot or wrinkle or anything like that, but holy and blameless. ²⁸ In the same way, husbands are to love their wives as their own bodies. He who loves his wife loves himself. ²⁹ For no one ever hates his own flesh but provides and cares for it, just as Christ does for the church, ³⁰ since we are members of his body. ³¹ For this reason a man will leave his father and mother and be joined to his wife, and the two will become one flesh. ³² This mystery is profound, but I am talking about Christ and the church. ³³ To sum up, each one of you is to love his wife as himself, and the wife is to respect her husband.

## EPHESIANS 6:1-9

### CHILDREN AND PARENTS

¹ Children, obey your parents in the Lord, because this is right. ² Honor your father and mother, which is the first commandment with a promise,

³ so that it may go well with you and that you may have a long life in the land. ⁴ Fathers, don't stir up anger in your children, but bring them up in the training and instruction of the Lord.

SLAVES AND MASTERS

⁵ Slaves, obey your human masters with fear and trembling, in the sincerity of your heart, as you would Christ. ⁶ Don't work only while being watched, as people-pleasers, but as slaves of Christ, do God's will from your heart. ⁷ Serve with a good attitude, as to the Lord and not to people, ⁸ knowing that whatever good each one does, slave or free, he will receive this back from the Lord. ⁹ And masters, treat your slaves the same way, without threatening them, because you know that both their Master and yours is in heaven, and there is no favoritism with him.

1 . Summarize Colossians 3:18–25 and 4:1 in one or two
sentences. What did you observe in today's reading?

2 . How does today's reading convict you?
How does it encourage you?

3 . How does today's reading from Colossians correct or
clarify your understanding of the gospel?

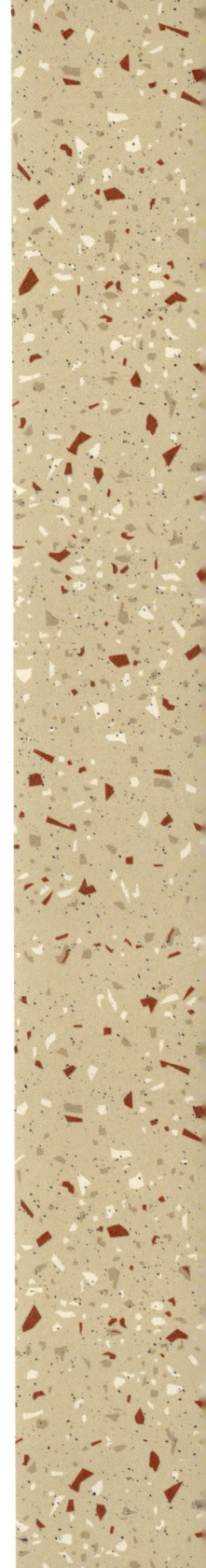

# MENTIONED BY NAME

It is a significant thing to be mentioned by name in the Bible. In Paul's epistles, he mentions many people by name. These men and women were real people—some brothers and sisters in Christ mentioned for their kingdom work, others mentioned because they opposed the work of the Church. Here are those whose names appear in the books of Colossians and Philemon.

## PAUL

Persecuted the early Church until he encountered the risen Christ. Apostle to the Gentiles, church planter, missionary, and friend to Onesimus.

COL 1:1
PHM 1, 16

## TIMOTHY

Disciple and traveling companion of Paul. Served churches in Corinth, Philippi, and Ephesus. Co-sender of several of Paul's letters.

COL 1:1
PHM 1
AC 16:1-4

## EPAPHRAS

A Colossian and faithful intercessor whom Paul called a "dearly loved fellow servant." Helped establish the church at Colossae and spread the gospel in Laodicea and Hierapolis.

COL 1:5-8; 4:12
PHM 23

## TYCHICUS

A man sent to encourage the Colossian church and deliver Paul's letter while the apostle was imprisoned. Minister and faithful servant of the gospel, whom Paul called a "dearly loved brother."

COL 4:7-8

## JESUS WHO IS CALLED JUSTUS

A Jewish man Paul mentions in his closing greetings to the Colossians.

COL 4:11

## LUKE

Author of the Gospel of Luke and the book of Acts. Close friend and ministry partner of Paul. Called "the dearly loved physician" and was with Paul during his final imprisonment.

COL 4:14
PHM 24
2TM 4:11

## DEMAS

A disciple who sent his greetings to the Colossians but later deserted Paul because he "loved this present world."

COL 4:14
PHM 24
2TM 4:10

## NYMPHA

A woman who held church services at her home.

COL 4:15

### ONESIMUS

Enslaved man who ran away from Philemon, then met Paul while Paul was imprisoned in Rome. Accompanied Tychicus to Colossae. Deeply appreciated by Paul and considered his son while he was in chains.

COL 4:9
PHM 8-22

### ARISTARCHUS

A Thessalonian man and Paul's traveling companion. Fellow prisoner with Paul in Rome who sent greetings to Philemon.

COL 4:10
PHM 24
AC 19:29; 20:4, 6

### MARK

Also known as John Mark. Author of the Gospel bearing his name. Traveled with Paul for the first missionary journey, but deserted him in Pamphylia. Was not invited to join the second missionary journey, but later rejoined Paul. Summoned by Paul during his final imprisonment and was recommended to others.

COL 4:10
PHM 23-24
AC 15:37-40
2TM 4:11

### ARCHIPPUS

A member of the Colossian church who received a ministry from the Lord. Referred to by Paul as "our fellow soldier." Possibly Philemon's son.

COL 4:17
PHM 2

### PHILEMON

A man who came to faith through Paul's ministry. The recipient of Paul's epistle of the same name and host of the church in Colossae.

PHM 1-2, 19

### APPHIA

A woman Paul mentions in his greeting to the Colossians. Likely Philemon's wife.

PHM 2

# Speaking to God and Others

**COLOSSIANS 4:2–18**

SPEAKING TO GOD AND OTHERS

[2] Devote yourselves to prayer; stay alert in it with thanksgiving. [3] At the same time, pray also for us that God may open a door to us for the word, to speak the mystery of Christ, for which I am in chains, [4] so that I may make it known as I should. [5] Act wisely toward outsiders, making the most of the time. [6] Let your speech always be gracious, seasoned with salt, so that you may know how you should answer each person.

FINAL GREETINGS

[7] Tychicus, our dearly loved brother, faithful minister, and fellow servant in the Lord, will tell you all the news about me. [8] I have sent him to you for this very purpose, so that you may know how we are and so that he may encourage your hearts. [9] He is coming with Onesimus, a faithful and dearly loved brother, who is one of you. They will tell you about everything here.

[10] Aristarchus, my fellow prisoner, sends you greetings, as does Mark, Barnabas's cousin (concerning whom you have received instructions: if

he comes to you, welcome him), [11] and so does Jesus who is called Justus. These alone of the circumcised are my coworkers for the kingdom of God, and they have been a comfort to me. [12] Epaphras, who is one of you, a servant of Christ Jesus, sends you greetings. He is always wrestling for you in his prayers, so that you can stand mature and fully assured in everything God wills. [13] For I testify about him that he works hard for you, for those in Laodicea, and for those in Hierapolis. [14] Luke, the dearly loved physician, and Demas send you greetings. [15] Give my greetings to the brothers and sisters in Laodicea, and to Nympha and the church in her home. [16] After this letter has been read at your gathering, have it read also in the church of the Laodiceans; and see that you also read the letter from Laodicea. [17] And tell Archippus, "Pay attention to the ministry you have received in the Lord, so that you can accomplish it."

[18] I, Paul, am writing this greeting with my own hand. Remember my chains. Grace be with you.

### PSALM 145:18-19

[18] The Lord is near all who call out to him,
all who call out to him with integrity.
[19] He fulfills the desires of those who fear him;
he hears their cry for help and saves them.

### PHILIPPIANS 4:6-7

[6] Don't worry about anything, but in everything, through prayer and petition with thanksgiving, present your requests to God.

[7] And the peace of God, which surpasses all understanding, will guard your hearts and minds in Christ Jesus.

1 .   Summarize Colossians 4:2-18 in one or two sentences.
       What did you observe in today's reading?

2 .   How does today's reading convict you?
       How does it encourage you?

3 .   How does today's reading from Colossians correct or
       clarify your understanding of the gospel?

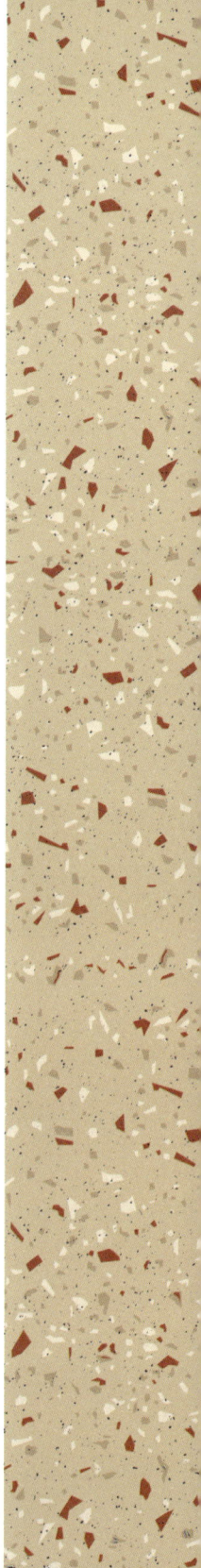

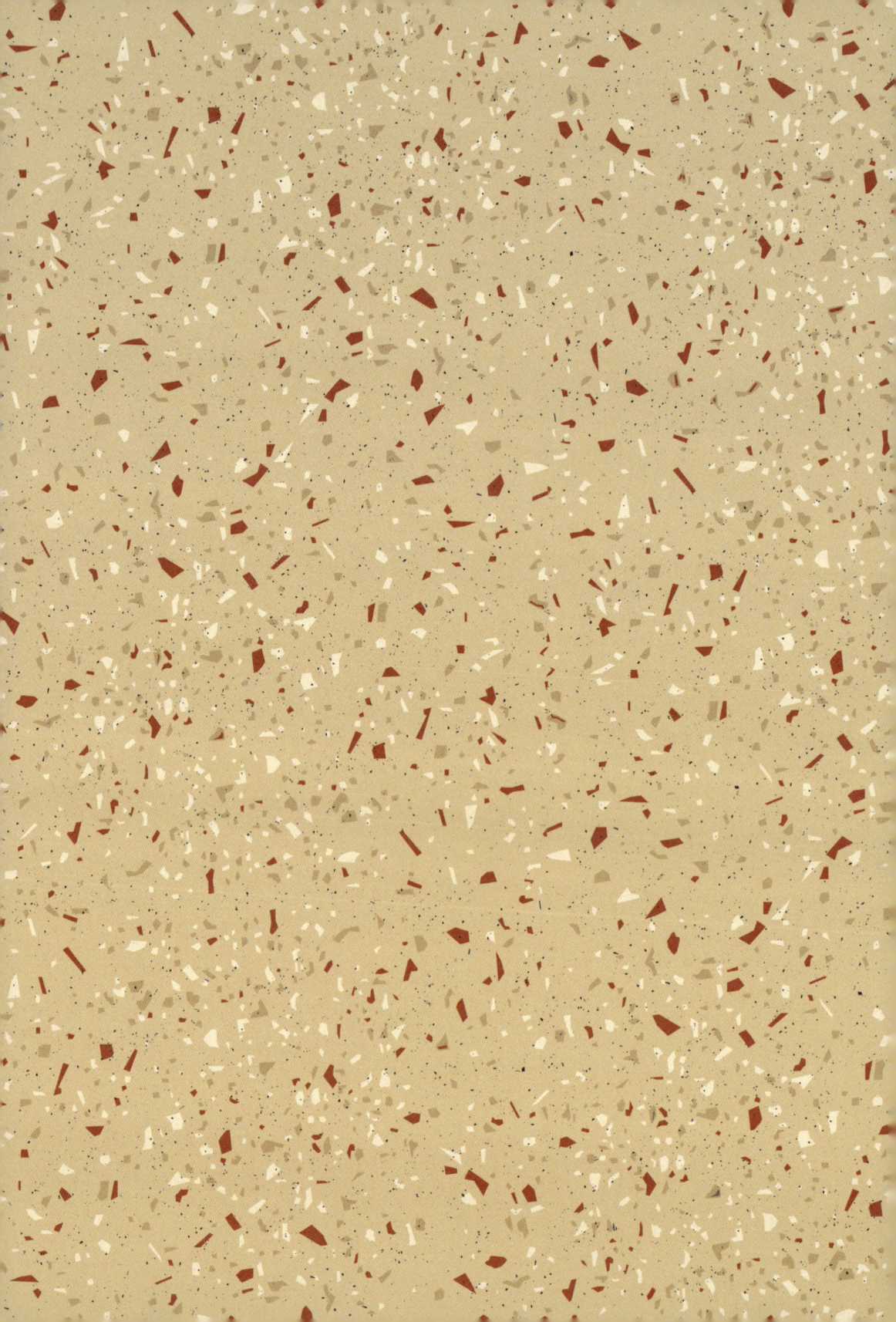

## ON THE TIMELINE

Paul's letter to Philemon was written during his imprisonment in Rome around AD 61. Philemon was written around the same time as Ephesians, Philippians, and Colossians after all three of Paul's missionary journeys.

## A LITTLE BACKGROUND

Philemon concerns a runaway slave, Onesimus, who had robbed his master, Philemon, and escaped from Colossae to Rome (Phm 15). Perhaps attracted by the anonymity of a large, distant city, Onesimus traveled to Rome seeking a life of freedom. While in Rome, he crossed paths with Paul and became a Christian (Phm 10, 16).

Paul wrote to Philemon about Onesimus and sent both the letter and Onesimus back to Colossae. In comparison to Paul's other letters, Philemon is little more than a postcard, but it comes from the tender heart of one friend writing to another, rather than an apostle exercising his authority.

## MESSAGE & PURPOSE

This letter has served as an inspiration for the liberation of slaves. Paul's clear preference was to keep Onesimus with him (Phm 13), but he recognized that Onesimus was legally bound to Philemon. Paul decided to send Onesimus back (Phm 12) so Philemon could either reinstate him as a slave who was now also his Christian brother (Phm 15-16), or set him free for further service to Paul back in Rome (Phm 13, 20-21). Onesimus returned to Philemon with this letter, knowing that Paul was confident of Philemon's "obedience" (Phm 21) but also knowing that forgiveness, reinstatement, and emancipation were not guaranteed.

## GIVE THANKS FOR THE BOOK OF PHILEMON

Although it is the shortest of Paul's letters, Philemon captures the heart of the gospel (Phm 16-19). When we come to God in repentance and faith, He gives us a new status and welcomes us as if we were Christ, who assumed personal responsibility for the full repayment of our debt to God.

# Philemon's Love and Faith

**PHILEMON 1-7**

GREETING

¹ Paul, a prisoner of Christ Jesus, and Timothy our brother:

To Philemon our dear friend and coworker, ² to Apphia our sister, to Archippus our fellow soldier, and to the church that meets in your home.

³ Grace to you and peace from God our Father and the Lord Jesus Christ.

PHILEMON'S LOVE AND FAITH

⁴ I always thank my God when I mention you in my prayers,

⁵ because I hear of your love for all the saints and the faith that you have in the Lord Jesus. ⁶ I pray that your participation in the faith may become effective through knowing every good thing that is in us for the glory of Christ. ⁷ For I have great joy and encouragement from your love, because the hearts of the saints have been refreshed through you, brother.

## PSALM 23

THE GOOD SHEPHERD

*A psalm of David.*

[1] The LORD is my shepherd;
I have what I need.
[2] He lets me lie down in green pastures;
he leads me beside quiet waters.
[3] He renews my life;
he leads me along the right paths
for his name's sake.
[4] Even when I go through the darkest valley,
I fear no danger,
for you are with me;
your rod and your staff—they comfort me.

[5] You prepare a table before me
in the presence of my enemies;
you anoint my head with oil;
my cup overflows.
[6] Only goodness and faithful love will pursue me
all the days of my life,
and I will dwell in the house of the LORD
as long as I live.

## PHILIPPIANS 1:3–11

THANKSGIVING AND PRAYER

[3] I give thanks to my God for every remembrance of you, [4] always praying with joy for all of you in my every prayer, [5] because of your partnership in the gospel from the first day until now. [6] I am sure of this, that he who started a good work in you will carry it on to completion until the day of Christ Jesus. [7] Indeed, it is right for me to think this way about all of you, because I have you in my heart, and you are all partners with me in grace, both in my imprisonment and in the defense and confirmation of the gospel. [8] For God is my witness, how deeply I miss all of you with the affection of Christ Jesus. [9] And I pray this: that your love will keep on growing in knowledge and every kind of discernment, [10] so that you may approve the things that are superior and may be pure and blameless in the day of Christ, [11] filled with the fruit of righteousness that comes through Jesus Christ to the glory and praise of God.

1. Summarize Philemon 1–7 in one or two sentences. What did you observe in today's reading?

2. How does today's reading convict you? How does it encourage you?

3. This short yet personal letter to Philemon captures the heart of the gospel. How does today's reading strengthen your understanding of how you are called to live differently because of the gospel?

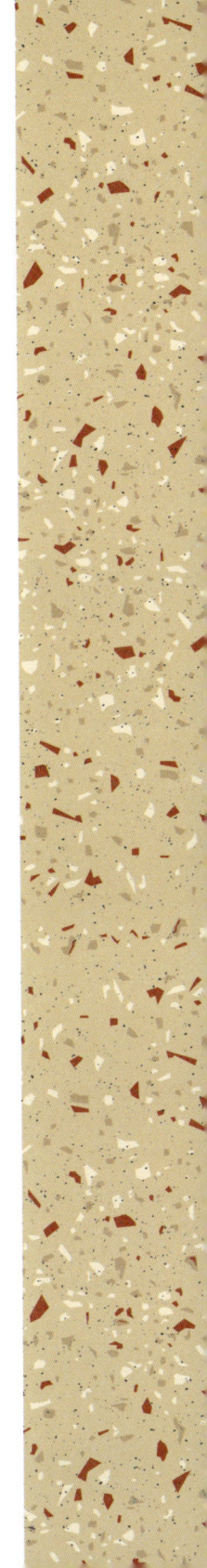

# An Appeal for Onesimus

**PHILEMON 8–25**

**AN APPEAL FOR ONESIMUS**   ·

[8] For this reason, although I have great boldness in Christ to command you to do what is right, [9] I appeal to you, instead, on the basis of love. I, Paul, as an elderly man and now also as a prisoner of Christ Jesus, [10] appeal to you for my son, Onesimus. I became his father while I was in chains. [11] Once he was useless to you, but now he is useful both to you and to me. [12] I am sending him back to you—I am sending my very own heart. [13] I wanted to keep him with me, so that in my imprisonment for the gospel he might serve me in your place. [14] But I didn't want to do anything without your consent, so that your good deed might not be out of obligation, but of your own free will. [15] For perhaps this is why he was separated from you for a brief time, so that you might get him back permanently, [16] no longer as a slave, but more than a slave—as a dearly loved brother. He is especially so to me, but how much more to you, both in the flesh and in the Lord.

[17] So if you consider me a partner, welcome him as you would me. [18] And if he has wronged you in any way, or owes you anything, charge that to my account. [19] I, Paul, write this with my own hand: I will repay it—not to mention to you that you owe me even your very self. [20] Yes, brother, may I benefit from you in the Lord;

refresh my heart in Christ.

[21] Since I am confident of your obedience, I am writing to you, knowing that you will do even more than I say. [22] Meanwhile, also prepare a guest room for me, since I hope that through your prayers I will be restored to you.

FINAL GREETINGS

[23] Epaphras, my fellow prisoner in Christ Jesus, sends you greetings, and so do [24] Mark, Aristarchus, Demas, and Luke, my coworkers.

[25] The grace of the Lord Jesus Christ be with your spirit.

## GENESIS 50:15-20

JOSEPH'S KINDNESS

[15] When Joseph's brothers saw that their father was dead, they said to one another, "If Joseph is holding a grudge against us, he will certainly repay us for all the suffering we caused him."

[16] So they sent this message to Joseph, "Before he died your father gave a command: [17] 'Say this to Joseph: Please forgive your brothers' transgression and their sin—the suffering they caused you.' Therefore, please forgive the transgression of the servants of the God of your father." Joseph wept when their message came to him. [18] His brothers also came to him, bowed down before him, and said, "We are your slaves!"

[19] But Joseph said to them, "Don't be afraid. Am I in the place of God? [20] You planned evil against me; God planned it for good to bring about the present result—the survival of many people."

**2 CORINTHIANS 5:16-17**

THE MINISTRY OF RECONCILIATION

[16] From now on, then, we do not know anyone from a worldly perspective. Even if we have known Christ from a worldly perspective, yet now we no longer know him in this way. [17] Therefore, if anyone is in Christ, he is a new creation; the old has passed away, and see, the new has come!

**GALATIANS 3:28**

There is no Jew or Greek, slave or free, male and female; since you are all one in Christ Jesus.

1.  Summarize Philemon 8–25 in one or two sentences.
    What did you observe in today's reading?

2.  How does today's reading convict you?
    How does it encourage you?

3.  How does today's reading strengthen
    your understanding of how you are called to
    live differently because of the gospel?

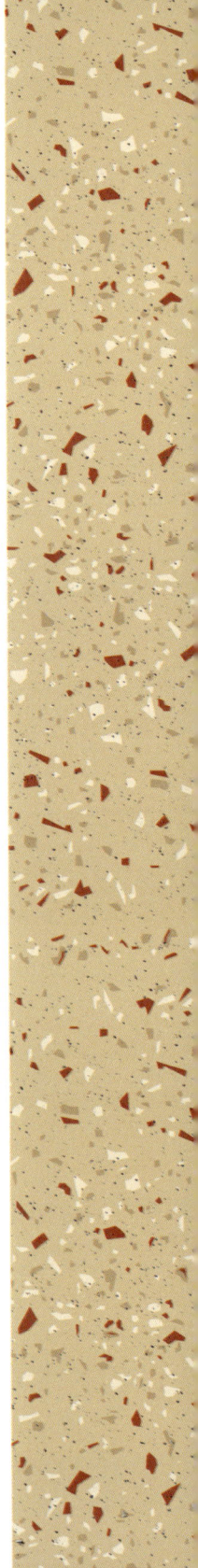

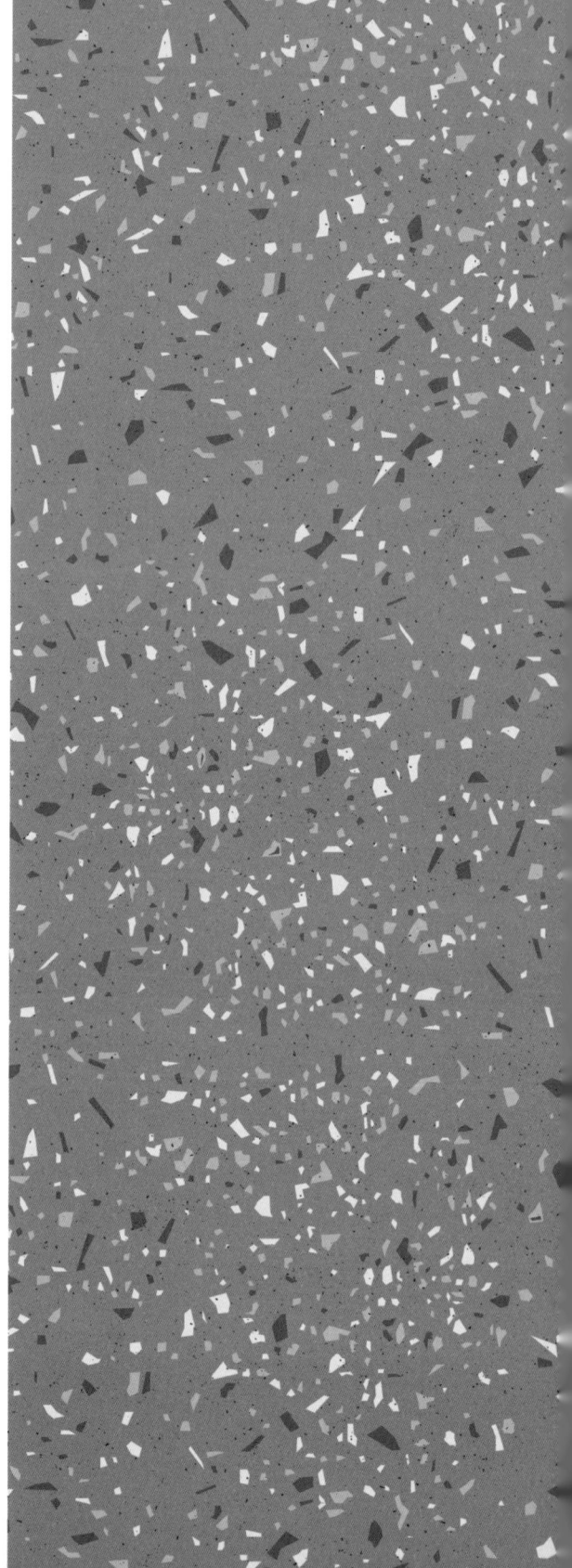

# Grace
# Day

Take this day to catch up on
your reading, pray, and rest in
the presence of the Lord.

The LORD is near all
who call out to him,
all who call out to
him with integrity.

PSALM 145:18

8 For this reason, although I have great boldness in Christ to command you to do what is right, 9 I appeal to you, instead, on the basis of love.

PHILEMON 8-9

# Weekly Truth

Scripture is God-breathed and true. When we memorize it, we carry the good news of Jesus with us wherever we go.

This week, memorize this key passage from the book of Philemon about Paul's desire for Philemon to accept his friend Onesimus. Say verse 8 aloud a few times and then add verse 9.

BENEDICTION

The grace of the
Lord Jesus Christ be
with your spirit.

PHILEMON 25

## CSB BOOK ABBREVIATIONS

**BIBLIOGRAPHY**

Barry, John D., Douglas Mangum, Derek R. Brown, Michael S. Heiser, Miles Custis, Elliot Ritzema, Matthew M. Whitehead, Michael R. Grigoni, and David Bomar. *Faithlife Study Bible*. Bellingham: Lexham Press, 2016.

Freedman, David Noel, Allen C. Myers, and Astrid B. Beck. *Eerdmans Dictionary of the Bible*. Grand Rapids: Wm. B. Eerdmans Publishing Company, 2000.

# LOOKING FOR HE READS TRUTH DEVOTIONALS?

Download the **He Reads Truth app** to find devotionals that complement your daily Scripture reading. If you're stuck on a passage, hop into the community discussion to instantly connect with other men who are reading with you. You can also download free lock screens for Weekly Truth memorization—all on the He Reads Truth app.

Want access to our entire library of reading plans? Subscribe to the **He Reads Truth Subscription Box** and you'll have free premium app access included with your subscription.

Visit HeReadsTruth.com/Subscription to learn more.

**DOWNLOAD THE HE READS TRUTH APP TODAY!**

## Where did I study?

- ☐ HOME
- ☐ OFFICE
- ☐ CHURCH
- ☐ SCHOOL
- ☐ COFFEE SHOP
- ☐ OTHER:

_____

_____

## What was I listening to?

SONG: _____

ARTIST: _____

ALBUM: _____

_____

## When did I study?
- ☐ MORNING
- ☐ AFTERNOON
- ☐ NIGHT

_____

_____

## What was happening in the world?

_____

_____

_____

_____

## What was happening in my life?

_____

_____

_____

_____

_____

_____

## How did I find delight in God's Word?

_____

END DATE

_____ / _____ / _____